# DRIVING PRACTICE WITH YOUR TEENAGER

## SAVE TIME, PETROL AND STRESS

**Jim Scotby**

**Paperback Edition**
**ISBN 978-1-905308-23-X**

**Published by Dawn Skies Publishing,**
**Southampton 19 SO15 5FY**
**info@dawnskiespublishing**

## Copyright, Trademarks and Disclaimer

## CONTENTS

# PART ONE:

# SETTING THE SCENE FOR YOU

## 1 Safe, effective and enjoyable...

Welcome to **DRIVING PRACTICE WITH YOUR TEENAGER.**

This book is aimed primarily at parents whose teenager is having paid driving lessons with a professional driving instructor.

The time will come when it makes sense for Mum or Dad to go out with "the Pupil" in the family car, to give him or her extra driving practice before the Practical Driving Test.

But on today's busy roads, and with today's demanding Practical Driving Test, there is rather more to these practice driving sessions than meets the eye.

That is where **DRIVING PRACTICE WITH YOUR TEENAGER** comes in - to make your driving practice sessions as safe, effective and enjoyable as possible, for both of you.

So here's hoping for a good few hours of driving practice together. May those hours play their part in achieving competent driving standards and a straightforward Practical Test pass.

To emphasise that your driving sessions have a serious purpose rather than just a "we might go for a spin some time" approach, we will refer to your teenager from now on as your "Pupil".

## 2 "When should we start on private practice?"

a) Be patient! Let your Pupil have several hours of paid lessons first.

b) Ask the Instructor to let you know when your Pupil is ready for private practice.

c) You might also ask if you can sit in on one or two driving lessons - you can see where your Pupil is "at" in their driving, and you can see how the Instructor actually handles a typical driving session.

## 3 CHECKLIST - Getting set up at the start

Before you take your Pupil out on the road in your own car, you must make sure you are "on side" concerning all these points:

### 1) All About You:

a) You must hold a full driving licence valid for the type of vehicle to be used for the instruction.

b) You must have held this full licence for at least three years.

c) You realise that you are responsible for the safety of your Pupil and yourself, of your vehicle, of other road users and other vehicles.

d) If an offence is committed during instruction, you realise that you are the one who is ultimately responsible.

### 2) All About Your Pupil:

a) Your Pupil must possess a valid Provisional Licence before being allowed to drive.

b) The holder of a Provisional Licence may only drive a vehicle when accompanied by, and under the supervision of, a driver who holds a full licence for that type of vehicle.

c) Your Pupil must be able to read the current style of number plate at a distance of 20 metres (22 yards / 66 feet).

d) If glasses or contact lenses are needed to achieve this, then these must be worn at all times when driving.

e) If there are any other concerns about eyesight, or other medical conditions, or disability, which might possibly affect your Pupil's driving ability and performance, check-ups at an optician and doctor are strongly advised.

The Law says the DVLA must be informed if your Pupil suffers from any serious medical condition. If in any doubt, please consult your doctor.

f) Check any medicines being taken for possible side-effects, such as drowsiness which might in turn affect driving ability.

g) Alcohol and driving, and drugs and driving, do not mix. If you have any fears over this concerning your own Pupil, you need to spell out this obvious fact with him or her before you go out together on the road.

**3) All About the Car**

The car you will be using for practising is probably a family car without dual controls. Here are some important points:

a) It is preferably a fairly small car, neither brand new nor very old.

b) A manual gearbox. (A Test can be taken in an automatic car, but in such a case your Pupil remains unlicensed to drive a manual car).

c) The car should preferably be "basic" in terms of engine size and performance; eg no greater than, say. 1.4 litres, and not "hotted-up".

d) The car should be in a safe and reliable condition, and have been recently serviced. Lights, tyres, wipers and blades, brakes etc must all be in good condition.

e) It must have a current road tax disc and MOT certificate.

f) It must be properly insured for your Pupil to drive it.

g) It is necessary for the Instructor to fit a second rear-view mirror, for use from the passenger seat. (Held in position by suction pad; you can buy one of these from eg Halfords).

h) Two side mirrors are also necessary, perhaps with a small extra "blind-spot" mirror attached to each if required.

i) Seat belts must be fitted and be in good condition.

j) L plates must be clearly displayed, visible from the front and rear of the car.

k) You might like to have dual controls fitted.

This is not as "way out" as it may sound! – especially if you are going to keep the car, and use it for subsequent children in years to come.

The cost of fitting such pedals is approximately £400 for cars such as Fiestas or Corsas, and the peace of mind you will both gain from their presence could well be worth the expenditure.

They can be removed later on if required. The most well-known company supplying dual controls is He-Man Equipment Ltd, Cable Street, Southampton, SO14 5AR, telephone 02380 226952. I understand that their parts can be fitted to cars by qualified fitters in different parts of the country, so you do not have to take the car all the way to Southampton.

Another firm is Bestway, in Birmingham, tel 0121 328 6226.

## 4 CHECKLIST - Basic Support Materials

a) **DRIVING PRACTICE WITH YOUR TEENAGER** is best used alongside the Highway Code and various other recommended titles.

The Highway Code concentrates only on the vital, basic "Rules of the Road". These of course are central and essential – but they do not tell the whole story. There is far more to driving safely than is covered in the Highway Code!

So do your best to make sure that your Pupil's copy of the Highway Code comes to be dog-eared and well-thumbed, as your Pupil thoroughly gets to know its contents.

b) Alongside the Highway Code I recommend you and your Pupil also make good use of the following titles:

- **"Know Your Traffic Signs"**
- **"Driving - The Essential Skills""**
- **"The Official Driving Test"**

c) Here are some further DSA publications which could also be useful:

- **The Official Guide to Learning to Drive**
- **The Official Guide to Helping Learners to Practise**

The above titles may be purchased online from these websites: www.tso.co.uk/bookshop (or) www.dsa.gov.uk.

## 5 Clashes of Opinion!

Bear in mind that, when driving, your Pupil is stuck between the proverbial "rock and a hard place" - the rock being the Instructor, and the hard place being you!

Your Pupil is becoming a competent driver, and will be keen to impress you and to hear you say "Well done".

You, for your part, I am sure, are a (usually!) competent driver, with a great deal more driving experience than your teenaged Pupil. But as you will be the first to agree, your knowledge of the Practical Driving Test is probably stuck in the proverbial time-warp of twenty years' ago. Life is very different now.

In addition, you are the parent of your Pupil, with all the family vibes that that may bring into play; you are using your car, in your freely-given time, you are shelling out serious money for the extra insurance, and you have no dual control pedals.

As such it is no surprise if your basic approach becomes, "Listen kid, just do as I say"!

So the scene is set.

Both you and the Instructor will be telling your Pupil what to do and what not to do, but you as the parent are probably not saying the same thing as the professional Instructor.

It is not surprising therefore that clashes of opinion as to what is correct driving practice are likely to arise between you and your Pupil, who of course will be relying more on what the Instructor has been saying than on what you are saying. That can hurt!

Result? - possible confusion, friction, ill-temper, and added danger. Nobody wants this.

So if you are in doubt over any driving issue, ask your Pupil to explain what the Instructor has taught, and go along with that. If you are still troubled over any such issue, just ask your Pupil's Instructor for an Official Ruling, and stick to that together.

Ultimately if your driving practice sessions are becoming a negative hassle for either of you, drop them. Leave them. No guilt - just accept that they are not working for whatever reason, and move on. Many Pupils pass the Practical Driving Test with no extra parental driving practice.

Such sessions are of course helpful if they are positive times for parent and Pupil, but they are not essential. It is well worth you both bearing that in mind.

# PART TWO:

# WHAT THE EXAMINERS ARE LOOKING FOR -

# YOUR REFRESHER COURSE ON TODAY'S PRACTICAL DRIVING TEST

It is very helpful for you to have a clear understanding of today's Practical Driving Test, which is markedly different from the Test you will have taken a good few years ago! There is obviously far more traffic today, and hence far more pressure on all drivers, irrespective of their age or experience.

It is sobering to realise that most drivers on today's UK roads would not pass the Practical Test that your Pupil is seeking to pass.

So here goes -

## 1 The Marking of the Test

The Examiner marks the Test Candidate's drive with four types of Fault:

a) **"Driving Fault":** the Candidate can have 15 such faults or less, and still pass the Test.

For example:

Poor use of side mirrors / Dodgy signals / Rough use of controls / Erratic steering / Poor observation / Going slightly too fast for a short distance / Going too slowly for the conditions / Getting too close to parked vehicles on the left (= "Clearance to Obstruction")

b) **"Serious Fault":** One such fault and the Candidate fails.

For example:

Any of the above faults if the consequences were, or were about to be, serious / Not coping well with meeting and passing oncoming traffic / Driving either too fast or too slowly for a considerable time /

Lack of awareness of other road users / Lane wanderings at roundabouts

c) **"Dangerous Fault":** One such fault and the Candidate fails.

For example:

Any of the above faults if the consequences were, or were about to be, dangerous / Any aspect of the Candidate's driving that the Examiner reports as dangerous.

(The Examiner's ultimate response is to stop the Test out on the Test route somewhere. He then says, "I am terminating this Test because it is too dangerous". He gets out, walks off, and makes his own way back to the Test Centre. The Candidate is "snookered", because he or she is not allowed to drive the car without a full licence holder being present. Somebody has to come out as a rescue party!).

d) **"Habitual Fault":** If at the end of the Test the Candidate has four Driving Faults in the same box for the same fault, this is called a "habitual fault". The Examiner will probably make these four little repeated faults into a Serious fault – which is enough to fail the Test.

## 2 The Topics on which a Candidate is assessed

On the next page is shown a list of each of the headings on the Examiner's Test Report sheet, beside which he will mark the type of Fault that he sees - Driving, Serious or Dangerous - as the Test proceeds.

Notice that there is nothing "nice" on the sheet; a perfect drive would show up as an empty sheet. So if on the Test the Candidate is aware that the Examiner is frequently marking the Test Report sheet, he or she needn't think "Ooh, aren't I doing well?". I am afraid it is just the opposite!

Eyesight
Maintenance
Cockpit drill
Ancillary controls

Controls:
Accelerator
Clutch
Gears
Foot brake
Hand brake
Steering

Judgement:
Overtaking
Meeting traffic
Crossing traffic

Response to signs/signals:
Traffic signs
Road markings
Traffic lights
Traffic controllers
Other road users

Use of mirrors:
Signalling
Changing direction

Changing speed

Give appropriate signals:
Where necessary
Correctly
Properly timed

Move away:
Safely
Under control

Junctions:
Approach speed
Observation
Turning right
Turning left
Cutting corners

Use of speed

Maintain progress by:
Driving at an appropriate speed
Avoiding undue hesitation

Positioning:
Normal driving
Lane discipline

Following distance
Clearance to obstructions

Awareness and Planning

Pedestrian crossings

Position for normal stops

Emergency stop:
Promptness
Control

Reverse to left:
Control
Observation

Turn in the road:
Control
Observation

Bay / Parallel parking:
Control
Observation

"Independent" driving
"Eco-friendly" driving

## 3 Safety and Courtesy

The Examiners are particularly keen on a Candidate's driving not affecting any other road user in a negative way. Some examples:

a) Emerging from a junction, or turning right across approaching traffic, causing oncoming vehicles to slow down or change direction.

b) Rolling back on a hill start, with another vehicle close behind.

c) Pulling away too soon before a pedestrian crossing is properly clear.

d) Being thoughtless on manoeuvres, causing delay or nuisance.

e) Not yielding when meeting traffic, when it is the Candidate's responsibility to have done so.

f) General thoughtlessness, selfishness, or lack of awareness.

## 4 Ten of the Most Common Reasons for Test Fails

According to recent DSA figures, here are ten of the most common reasons for failing the Practical Driving Test.

a) Poor observation at junctions.

b) Poor control or observation on the bay park.

c) Poor use of mirrors, or not acting properly on the information within those mirrors.

d) Poor control or observation on the left reverse.

e) Incorrect signals, such as not being cancelled, or being misleading.

f) Moving away unsafely eg no signal or blind spot check.

g) Poor positioning, especially for roundabouts and bends.

h) Poor steering - erratic, hasty, etc.

i) Poor positioning for turning right, at junctions and in One-Way streets.

j) Too low a speed, with hesitancy

## 5 "Independent Driving"

This lasts 5 – 10 minutes during the Test, and is designed to check that the Candidate can drive safely without being given directions all the time.

The Examiner will ask the Candidate:

**EITHER** a) to follow road signs to a particular place;

**OR** b) to follow short routes involving two or three junctions, which he either shows on a simple diagram, or describes to the Candidate, whichever the Candidate requests when asked;

**OR** c) a mixture of a) and b).

It is very important to remember that the diagrams are NOT TO SCALE. They ONLY SHOW JUNCTIONS. They do NOT show distance, and they do NOT show wiggly roads.

## 6 "Eco-Friendly Driving"

The Examiner is looking to see that the controls are used smoothly and correctly throughout the drive, to save fuel, to save wear and tear on the car, and to give a calm ride for the occupants of the car.

In each case we are looking for the "Goldilocks Touch" - not too much, not too little, but just about right.

This "eco-friendly driving" applies especially to:

- **the accelerator pedal** - enough "gas" but not too much
- **the brake pedal** - smooth, gentle, applied in good time

- **the clutch** - especially that the clutch is smoothly lifted up when your Pupil has dropped from a higher gear to a lower gear

- **the gears** - correct selection of gears in view of the speed and position of the car, to ensure most economical use of fuel and to avoid the risk of stalling

- **the steering wheel** - smoothly turned, correctly timed, with "slidey hands", that is, with neither hand going over the top of the steering wheel to the other side when the car is being steered to one side or the other

- **the attitude of your Pupil** when driving - calm, moderate, confident without being cocky, in control, courteous.

## 7 The Reversing Manoeuvres

On the Practical Driving Test the Candidate will be asked to carry out one of the following reversing manoeuvres:

**Turn in the Road / Left Reverse / Bay Park / Parallel Park**

For any manoeuvre your Pupil should apply the following key word:

**C O G S!**

**C stands for Control:** The Examiner is looking for full control of the car throughout the manoeuvre.

**O stands for Observation:** The Examiner is looking for thorough observation all around the car throughout the manoeuvre

**G and S stand for GO SLOW:**

**Your Pupil MUST GO SLOW** from start to finish of the manoeuvre, to give time for proper control and for proper observation.

## 1 THE TURN IN THE ROAD

The Examiner tells the Candidate to pull up at the side of the road in a place chosen by the Examiner.

He then says something like this - "I'd like you to carry out a turn in the road, to turn the car round to face in the opposite direction. Try not to hit the kerbs or driveways".

COGS: Control / Observation / GO SLOW

**Test Requirements**

a) Turn the car round to face in the opposite direction.

b) Do not hit the kerb.

c) Demonstrate full control.

d) Demonstrate effective observation.

**Main Faults on the Turn in the Road:**

a) Hitting the kerb.

b) Poor observation.

c) Getting muddled between 1st and reverse gears.

d) Getting muddled about which way to steer.

## 2 THE LEFT REVERSE

The Examiner tells the Candidate to pull up at the side of the road before a side road on the left.

He then says something like this - "I'd now like you to carry out the left reverse manoeuvre. Please drive past the side road ahead of us here on the left. Stop the car beyond it, then reverse the car round into the side road, keeping reasonably close to the left hand kerb. Try not to hit the kerb or any driveway".

COGS: Control / Observation / GO SLOW

**Test Requirements**

a) Reverse the car round a left corner into a side road.

b) Do not hit the kerb.

c) Demonstrate full control.

d) Demonstrate effective observation.

**Main Faults on the Left Reverse:**

a) Hitting the kerb.

b) Swinging out too wide.

c) Poor observation.

## 3 THE BAY PARK, TO LEFT OR RIGHT

If this is the chosen reversing manoeuvre for the Test, it takes place in the Test Centre car park at the very start or at the very end of the Test.

The Examiner says something like this to the Candidate - "I'd now like you to carry out a reverse park manoeuvre. Please reverse into a bay of your choice".

Notice that the Candidate can choose the bay, and can choose whether to do a left hand turn or right hand turn into the chosen bay.

On this manoeuvre it is essential that there is some element of turning the steering wheel when reversing; ie., the Candidate cannot just swing forwards round to the right by 90 degrees, to be parallel to the bay lines behind the car, then reverse straight back into the bay.

COGS: Control / Observation / GO SLOW

**Test Requirements**

a) Reverse the car into a parking bay of your choice.
b) The car must be parked within the bay, not hitting the back kerb, not straddling either white line, and not protruding from the front of the bay.

c) Demonstrate full control.

d) Demonstrate effective observation.

**Main Faults on the Bay Park**

a) Poor observation.

b) Hitting the kerb or wall at the back.

c) Stopping when the front of the care is not yet in the bay.

d) Leaving one or more tyres on the wrong side of a white line.

## 4 THE PARALLEL PARK
## (also called "REVERSE PARK")

The Examiner tells the Candidate to pull up at the side of the road a couple of car lengths before a vehicle parked ahead on the left.

He then says something like this - "I'd now like you to carry out a reverse park manoeuvre. Please drive alongside the vehicle parked ahead of you, then reverse back into the space behind it within two car lengths, parking reasonably close to the left hand kerb. Try not to hit the kerb or any driveway. For the purposes of this manoeuvre you can park the car across a driveway".

COGS: Control / Observation / GO SLOW

**Test Requirements**

a) Reverse the car into a parking space behind another parked vehicle, within two car lengths.

b) Demonstrate full control.

c) Demonstrate effective observation.

**Main Faults on Parallel Park:**

a) Poor observation.

b) Hitting the kerb – or the parked car ....

c) Stopping not close enough in to the kerb.

## 8 The Emergency Stop

The Emergency Stop exercise is set only on every third or fourth Test, and is in addition to the reversing manoeuvre.

The Examiner tells the Candidate to pull up at the side of the road.

He then says something like this - "I'd now like you to carry out the emergency stop exercise which you have been practising with your Instructor. When you have driven off in a moment, I will check conditions are safe. When I raise my right hand with the instruction "STOP!" you must then stop the car promptly and under full control. Try not to anticipate my instruction. Have you got any questions? Please drive on when you are ready".

### Test Requirements

a) Bring the car to a prompt stop when signalled to do so.

b) Demonstrate full control.

c) Demonstrate effective observation when appropriate.

### Main Faults on Emergency Stop:

a) Not prompt.

b) Lack of control – such as braking too heavily causing a skid, or too little causing not stopping promptly, or erratic steering.

c) Clutch down at same time as brakes applied – thus “coasting”, leading to loss of engine’s compression to assist with braking, and less control of the car.

d) Poor observation when stopped.

e) Poor procedure when moving off – such as poor observation.

# PART THREE:

# HOW TO BE THE BEST POSSIBLE DRIVING PRACTICE PARENT FOR YOUR PUPIL

## 1 Your Job in a Nutshell - as you give driving practice to your Pupil

At the heart of all effective driving instruction is a basic three-fold task:

- **FAULT IDENTIFICATION: WHAT is the problem?**
- **FAULT ANALYSIS: WHY is the problem happening?**
- **FAULT REMEDY: HOW do we get rid of the problem?**

## 2 "Get out of the way!"

The input of the full licence holder, be it the professional Instructor or yourself, should be steadily reduced as the driving ability of your Pupil increases. Understanding the need for this “brain-swapping” process is vital for effective driving instruction.

The best driving sessions you will have together are when you are at the stage of hardly having to say anything, other than giving directions, because the quality of your Pupil’s driving is now leaving you with nothing to say.

"Silence - (on your part) - is golden!"

## 3 The Heart of all Good Driving - what to look for consistently

At all times you are looking for the following sequence of tasks, which lies at the heart of all safe driving. This is an improved version of the old "Mirror, Signal, Manoeuvre" routine you probably came across in your own driving lessons "all those years ago" -

- **Think Ahead**

- **Scan and Plan**
- **Mirror, Mirror, Signal**
- **Position, Speed, Gears**
- **Do the Job**
- **On to the Next**

**Think Ahead means -**
Keeping in mind the route you are following, and what you will do at the next junction - even before you can see it.

**Scan and Plan means -**
Staying far ahead of the car, mentally and visually, all the time, looking, seeing, expecting, anticipating.
This gives time and space to see, to react, to prepare.
This reduces the chance of being taken by surprise.

**Mirror, Mirror, Signal means -**
Checking your rear view mirror.
Checking the side mirror of the side you are concerned with.
Putting on the signal at the right time - not too soon or too late.

**Position, Speed, Gears means -**
Putting, or keeping, the car in the correct position on the road for the job to be done (eg to prepare for a right turn, the car is moved towards the centre line of the road, after proper mirrors and a signal).
Adjusting the speed of the car to what is necessary for the job to be done, which for any junctions will mean slowing down.
Selecting the best gear for the new speed. (Speed is always the first thing to get sorted; then the gears are sorted, to fit in with the speed).

**Do the Job means -**
Carrying out whatever job you have been preparing for, smoothly, calmly and safely.

**On to the Next means -**
Leaving that job behind, and Scanning and Planning for what is coming next.

Just remember another simple motto when it comes to consistency and safety -

- **No Surprises!**
- **No Surprises by Them for Us**
- **No Surprises for Them by Us**

## 4 Twelve Abilities for your Pupil to Develop

Getting slightly more technical for a moment, here is a useful list to keep in mind:

a) The ability to avoid risk, eg not to “race” another vehicle.

b) The ability to be confident but not cocky.

c) The ability to use visual scanning, eg being aware of what is happening, or is likely to happen, “around and about”.

d) The ability to have an appropriate width of vision, eg the habit of checking around and behind as well as ahead.

e) The ability to observe and obey traffic regulations, such as road signs and lane marking.

f) The ability to assess speed, distance, space and timing, eg oncoming traffic.

g) The ability to react in good time, eg seeing a problem situation ahead and taking appropriate action.

h) The ability to focus on priorities, eg keeping to an appropriate speed rather than chatting to a friend in the car.

i) The ability to divide attention across more than one simultaneous task.

j) The ability to use short-term memory, such as remembering what is in the mirrors.

k) The ability to change plans quickly and safely.

l) The ability to practise hand-eye co-ordination when using the controls.

## 5 How Long to Make the Driving Sessions

It depends.

Probably up to one hour is about right - long enough to get into the swing of it, but short enough to be fitted into busy lives with neither of you getting too tired.

## 6 Where To Go

It is much better not to try to concentrate on any supposed Test routes in your driving sessions with your Pupil. These routes, which are no longer published on the internet, are constantly being changed, in a bid by the Examiners to stay one step ahead of the professional Instructors.

Instead, concentrate on general driving in the Test area, and within that area, particularly on the "nasty places", some of which are very likely to crop up on the Test whichever Test route the Examiner chooses. Your Pupil will have come across many of these already on the driving lessons.

"Nasties" mean such places as large, busy roundabouts, major traffic lights junctions, dual carriageways, crowded shopping streets, one-way streets etc – any place which is going to demand extra care for any driver.

When practising the reversing manoeuvres, try to use quiet, wide roads, where the inconvenience caused to residents and other road users can be kept to a minimum.

## 7 Prepare Beforehand

Preparing properly makes a real difference:

a) Check what you covered last time: what went well or badly; and what you jotted down at the end of your last lesson with your Pupil as to what you thought should be covered this next time.

b) Have a good idea of any particular topics which need more attention and improvement by your Pupil, which you will try to work on together in this driving session.

c) Work out what to say, how and when to explain it, plus any possible diagrams you might draw yourself.

d) Think about the most suitable type of area and roads to make use of, bearing in mind your Pupil's ability, the time of day of the session, and the likely traffic conditions.

e) Arising from your preparation, now roughly put the session together in your mind, and perhaps jot it on to some paper, especially how long you plan to spend on each part of the session – and where.

f) Try to anticipate any problems, and any questions that may arise.

g) Practise talking it through yourself.

h) Perhaps practise it in the car by yourself, especially if it is something you are "iffy" about yourself!

## 8 Do Keep Notes

It is worth the effort of allocating a customised Driving Sessions Notebook to these driving sessions before you begin.

Keep it accessible and up-to-date. It will make all the difference to the standard of help you are giving to your Pupil.

At the end of every session, jot down such details as: what you did / where you went / successes and progress / weaknesses and struggles / and, particularly, suggestions for next session.

Then use those notes for next time! They will serve as a reminder of what you did, and of what you need to work on during this next driving practice session.

# PART FOUR:

# ALL ABOUT SAFETY ON YOUR DRIVING PRACTICE SESSIONS

Safety is obviously at the heart of all that you will be doing on your driving practice sessions. It deserves this section all to itself.

## SAFETY FIRST, SECOND AND ALWAYS!

**Let us define "a good driver" like this:**

**"A good driver is the one who comes safely home, and has helped all other road users to do the same"**

As the saying goes – "Safety is no accident". Safety must lie at the heart of all our driving.

Here are 20 vital "Dooz and Don'tz" to help you maintain safety on your driving practice sessions together:

**Your general approach:**

a) SAFETY FIRST Set and maintain a calm atmosphere in the car.

b) SAFETY FIRST Don't get bad tempered or over-excited. Sort out any crisis safely, then pull in and explain calmly what happened, and why, and what you did to sort it out.

c) SAFETY FIRST Be patient with other road users, and thank them for their patience with you.

d) SAFETY FIRST Admit your mistakes – but keep mistakes to a minimum so that your Pupil can still have confidence in you.

**Before you get into the car:**

d) SAFETY FIRST Remember your Pupil's limitations. In the light of these, plan roughly where you will be going and what you will be doing before you set out. Bear in mind the weather and light conditions, the time of day and the likely level of traffic.

**At the start of the drive:**

e) SAFETY FIRST Spend a minute or two discussing how things are going: any good points from last time; any iffy points from last time. Establish roughly what you will be doing this time.

f) SAFETY FIRST Ensure the Cockpit Drill is properly completed, for you both - seat position, mirrors, etc.

**On the drive:**

g) SAFETY FIRST Never, ever relax, but try to give off calm vibes.

h) SAFETY FIRST Keep alert at all times - constant awareness of what is going on ahead, around and behind the car.

i) SAFETY FIRST Expect the unexpected.

j) SAFETY FIRST Be ready to grab the steering wheel and call for brakes and clutch if necessary.

k) SAFETY FIRST Speak and act calmly and clearly, in good time.

l) SAFETY FIRST Keep materials on your knee to a minimum.

m) SAFETY FIRST Write nothing when the car is in motion, ever.

n) SAFETY FIRST Always look for yourself – never rely only on your Pupil's ability and judgement.

o) SAFETY FIRST "Back your own hunch" – if you are conscious of possible risk or danger, act on that sense.

p) SAFETY FIRST Look thoroughly to your right when about to emerge from any junction (as well as to the left of course) – the right side is the hardest place for you to see but is always the most important place to check.

q) SAFETY FIRST Keep planning ahead and adjust your plans if necessary depending on how things are going.

r) SAFETY FIRST Always keep a safe distance from the vehicle in front, bearing in mind the weather and road surface.

s) SAFETY FIRST Encourage the habit of steady, safe braking begun in good time.

t) SAFETY FIRST Come home safely.

**SO – your constant motto is just this:**

**BE PREPARED FOR**

***ANYTHING***

**AT**

***ANY TIME***

**Be especially prepared for any or all of these:**

- **A reluctance to slow down, give way or stop, usually because your Pupil does not see the need for such action.**
- **A tendency for your Pupil to over-react, such as a sudden braking, or a wrench of the steering wheel. EITHER OF THESE IS VERY DANGEROUS.**
- **A stall by your Pupil when attempting to move the car away, especially in more pressurised situations such as moving away at traffic lights or a roundabout.**

# PART FIVE: MIXING IT UP -

# KEEPING YOUR DRIVING PRACTICE SESSIONS EFFECTIVE AND FUN

## 1 Explanation and Experience

Try to blend explanation and experience:

Explanation alone – that is, you talking while the car is parked – is clearly not enough. Your Pupil needs to go out and do it.

But experience alone – your Pupil simply driving around following your off-the-cuff directions – is clearly not enough either: that could well be dangerous, as well as being poor use of time and petrol.

The phrase “active learning” is helpful. Keep your Pupil involved, engaged, participating, interested.

## 2 Diagrams, Sketches, and "Independent Driving"

Do you remember that old saying which goes something like this? “I hear and I forget; I see and I remember; I do and I understand”. This technique, of sketching out your own diagrams will greatly help your Pupil understand the points you are making. The more of these quick, rough sketches you can do, the better.

So I recommend you keep handy an A4 pad of blank paper and a pen.

You can use this technique for practising the "independent driving" junction diagrams. Pull in. Think where you are and how you can set a simple route ahead involving two or three junctions. Quickly draw a simple diagram showing this route, with short straight roads and the junctions.

Explain it, and get your Pupil to say it back to you. Then, off you go.

### 3 Model Cars

Another tip to assist your practice sessions is to use little model cars in your explanations. Again, this is all about visualisation to help your Pupil "see" as well as merely hear.

### 4 "Road Sign Tennis"

An excellent instructional technique to encourage your Pupil's awareness is to ask about any road signs you pass. You can turn this into a simple game of "Road Sign Tennis" perhaps:

a) Basic level - ask about any sign as you approach it: a point to your Pupil for every sign correctly identified, or a point to you if not.

b) Advanced level - ask about any sign after you have passed it: two points if your Pupil noticed it AND correctly identifies it

### 5 Give "a Demo"

It is often helpful to swap seats and carry out yourself what you may have just been explaining to your Pupil. Show them; drive the car in the way you have just been explaining. This is similar to a Commentary Drive - see below - but usually lasts less time and concentrates on one specific Topic.

### 6 "Commentary Driving"

This technique can be very helpful. Just drive yourself for a few minutes, giving a running commentary on all you are seeing, deciding and doing.

A Demo drive concentrates on one Topic, but this Commentary drive is more general.

A further form of commentary driving is to encourage your Pupil to give the commentary on his/her own driving – to speak aloud of things he or she is watching for, is seeing, is planning, is doing.

## 7 “Q & A”

Develop a "question and answer” approach to encourage your Pupil to think and scan and plan ahead.

For example:

"Which lane for this roundabout ...?" or -

"What gear for this junction ...? or -

"What did that driver in the blue car do well ...?" or -

"How could that bus driver have coped better with that situation?".

# PART SIX:

# SOME PRACTICAL SUGGESTIONS TO ACHIEVE CONSISTENCY

## 1 Giving Directions and Instructions

It is important to give directions and instructions in the proper format. This habit builds consistency for your Pupil, and prepares him or her for how the Examiner will speak on the Practical Test.

Be consistent in the words you use, your tone of voice and the timing of directional instructions.

b) Always use the same format:
Identify the place eg "At the traffic lights / roundabout / etc ...
Identify the direction eg "...turn left / right / follow the road ahead

c) Use Left, Right or Road Ahead, not Straight On...

d) For roundabouts, give the direction (Left, Right or Road Ahead), then the exit number. For example: "At the roundabout, turn right please, which is the third exit ....".

e) Add in a Please usually, but make sure this "does not get in the way" of the main message.

f) Give properly-timed directions:

When your Pupil can take it in and understand, ie not when your Pupil is halfway through something else.
When the carrying-out of the instruction is the next obvious task, ie soon enough for your Pupil's awareness and planning, but not too soon to clutter up their mind with detail they do not yet need.

g) Rarely give two instructions at once, unless the second is going to affect how they carry out the first. eg: "At the first roundabout follow the road ahead, then at the second roundabout, turn right, 3rd exit (this tips them off to leave the 1st roundabout into the right hand lane).

h) Be prepared to assist with choice of lane, unless your Pupil is very advanced.

i) Emphasise any key words.

j) Be prepared to repeat the direction.

k) Make sure your Pupil has reacted correctly, especially in terms of a correct Left or Right signal.

l) Some examples:

"At the roundabout, turn left please, 1st exit".
"At the roundabout, follow the road ahead – that's the 2nd exit".
"At the crossroads, turn right please".
"Please now pull in at a convenient place".
"At the traffic lights, we shall be turning left".
"Please take the second road on the right – this one (pointing at it as you approach and pass) being the first".
"Thank you …drive on when you are ready".
"Just beyond the bridge, there is a fork in the road. Take the left fork there please".

## 2 A Pupil Muddled with Left and Right

Get your Pupil simply to write an L and R on their hands – simple, but effective.

## 3 Giving Correction

This needs to be positive: point out errors certainly, but in a friendly way, with the solutions being offered to any mistakes that may have been made.

It also helps if correction is given promptly, so the events are still fresh in your Pupil's mind, and preferably when you have pulled in to the kerb.

But, while trying to be encouraging, you need to remain honest! Ultimately it is no help to your Pupil if you have constantly said how wonderful your Pupil is, when the reality is rather different. Affirm whenever possible, while also explaining how any "iffy" driving practices can be improved on the next occasion they arise.

## 4 Giving "Feedback"

Ask your Pupil frequently "How's it going?", "How did you feel about that roundabout?", "How did you feel the session went today?" and even, "How are you finding these sessions? What do you find helpful or difficult about the way I am going about things?"

React to what you hear – it will make your time together in the car more effective.

## 5 Changing Your Methods

Let me emphasise again that your approach should gradually change as your Pupil's skills and understanding improve.

You need to tailor your approach to the proficiency of your Pupil. Basically remember it means you trying to say less and less during a drive.

## 6 Mock Tests

Your Pupil will hopefully have one or more Mock Tests with his or her Driving Instructor, but there is much to be said for you doing the same, when the time is right.

PART TWO of this book has told you about the Practical Driving Test. You might like to print off the page showing the Test headings (page 15) to keep with you on your driving practice sessions.

There are two main advantages in having Mock Tests:

a) It shows you both what the Test is like. The "vibes" in the car on a Test are very different from those on a driving lesson with the Instructor or on a driving session with Mum or Dad.

b) It very quickly bubbles up to the surface any specific driving faults or weaknesses of attitude or response in your Pupil – which can then be addressed and eliminated.

The one snag with a full Mock Test is that you cannot deal at the time with any problems that may arise. Just as on the real Practical Driving Test, on a Mock Test you, as the Examiner, will only give a report on the drive at the very end of the Test.

To get round that, you can go for the "halfway house" of "Test conditions".

## 7 "Test Conditions"

When your Pupil is ready, rather than have a full and formal Mock Test each session, you can agree that the Pupil is to drive under "Test conditions".

This means you both behave as if the Pupil is indeed on a Mock Test, so you, like a Test Examiner, are not going to give any help to the Pupil as the drive proceeds, beyond giving directions and instructions about pulling in and so on.

However, if and when your Pupil makes a mistake, you can immediately announce the Fault you are giving - Driving, Serious or Dangerous. If appropriate you can pull in and go through the incident together right there and then.

This has the great advantage of immediacy. It is much easier for the Pupil to learn from the situation right at the time, rather than you both having to wait until the end of a Test before you can go through together what happened. By that stage there will be other faults to deal with as well.

So best of all, try to have a blend of approach on your driving sessions, from normal help-being-given-while-driving, through Test conditions, to the occasional formal Mock Test where you fill in the Test sheet "as for real".

Where you are on that blend will depend very much on your Pupil's driving ability.

## 8 Any Queries – Ask your Pupil's Instructor

Both you and the Instructor are on the same side – wanting to make your Pupil a safe, competent driver ready to pass the Practical Test.

So work together as allies whenever necessary. If you have any questions over current "best driving practice", just ask your Pupil's Instructor to help you out.

# PART SEVEN:

# PULLING IT ALL TOGETHER -

# A TYPICAL DRIVING PRACTICE SESSION

Pulling it all together, here is a useful sequence which can be used as a basic "template" for most sessions – but again, bear in mind the need to be flexible if appropriate.

This may be more systematic than suits you or your Pupil, in which case just use the bits you like the look of.

In all that follows here, you won't go far wrong if you just remember - "Do it with a KISS!" Keep It Short and Simple!

## 1 At the start

a) Prompt, friendly and cheerful!

b) Have your Notebook ready and waiting – which demonstrates that you are well-organised.

c) The car to be in good condition.

d) Check your Pupil is OK; (because if he or she is not OK, for whatever reason, it will affect their driving, and you need to know before the lesson gets started).

e) Settle your Pupil into the car, assist as necessary with the cockpit drill.

## 2 Recap / Objective / Briefing

a) Remind what you have covered already in previous sessions together.

b) If you want to work on anything specific this time, emphasise especially any Topic you have already covered which leads on into this one, (eg reversing last time, leading on to, say, the Left Reverse manoeuvre this time).

c) Objective: What you are going to tackle this time, and how.

d) Briefing: Explain any Topic from your point of view, in the light of what your Pupil may already have done on this with the professional Instructor. Answer any questions.

**3 Demo drive or Commentary drive?**

**4 Your Pupil's turn**

**5 Debriefs during, as appropriate**

a) Pull the car over and stop somewhere safe, legal and convenient.

b) Talk things through – how is it going; any problems; any driving situations which you have just encountered - what happened and why; how to be solved.

**6 Changes of emphasis**

a) Perhaps change activity now for a few minutes.

b) Be sensitive. Don't "overflog" a Topic, especially if your Pupil is getting stressed with it.

**7 At the end of the session**

a) Debrief again as necessary

b) Discuss general progress and any concerns on either side. Update your notes from this session, with suggestions for the next session.

c) Update together, after every few sessions, the Driver Record Sheet (at the end of this book, for you to photocopy, if you want to use that).

This is a chance for mutual honesty, and mutual re-focussing as and when necessary.

d) Sort out a date and time for your next driving practice session together, which emphasises to you both that these sessions matter and are being taken seriously.

# PART EIGHT:

# ONE VERY LAST THING

A final word for that patient, long-suffering parent instructor, who has given many hours to your Pupil in the noble cause of extra driving practice.

In the midst of all that you are trying to remember and put into practice for your Pupil's sake, above all, try to enjoy these driving sessions!

Besides being very useful and helpful for your Pupil, these times can also be fun, especially when you look back on them in times to come.

They will make you both better drivers, and will hopefully bring you much closer to one another than you were before.

**So go for it together. Keep smiling – and keep safe.**

## SAMPLE TEMPLATE
## DRIVER'S RECORD SHEET for your Pupil

(Suggestion: Print a copy. Fill in, with Pupil, after every few sessions)
1=full instruction; 2=prompted; 3=seldom prompted; 4=independence

| | |
|---|---|
| Controls:<br>Move away:<br>Position for normal stops<br>Cockpit drill:<br><br>Response to signs/signals:<br><br>Use of mirrors:<br>Signalling<br>Changing direction<br>Changing speed<br><br>Give appropriate signals:<br>Where necessary<br>Correctly<br>Properly timed<br><br>Junctions:<br>Approach speed<br>Observation<br>Turning right<br>Turning left<br>Cutting corners<br><br>Positioning:<br>Normal<br>Lane discipline<br>(Changing lane)<br>(Bus lane) | Clearance to obstructions<br>Following distance<br><br>Use of speed:<br>Maintain progress by:<br>Appropriate speed<br>Hesitation<br><br>Aware / Planning /Judgement:<br><br>Meeting traffic<br>Crossing traffic<br>Overtaking<br><br>Pedestrian Crossings<br><br>Maintenance:<br>Ancillary controls<br><br>Manoeuvres:<br>Turn in the Road:<br>Left Reverse<br>Bay Park<br>Parallel Park<br>Emergency Stop<br><br>Independent driving:<br>Road signs<br>Junction diagrams |

## INDEX

# DRIVING PRACTICE WITH YOUR TEENAGER

## SAVE TIME, PETROL AND STRESS

**Jim Scotby**

**Paperback Edition**
**ISBN 978-1-905308-23-X**

**Published by Dawn Skies Publishing,**
**Southampton 19 SO15 5FY**
**info@dawnskiespublishing**

www.ingramcontent.com/pod-product-compliance
Ingram Content Group UK Ltd.
Pitfield, Milton Keynes, MK11 3LW, UK
UKHW051308070726
13610UKWH00013B/73